Spirits of the Texas Revolution:
A Book of Texan Poetry

Spirits of the Texas Revolution: A Book of Texan Poetry

By Betsy Wagner

Illustrations by Susan Walrath Pape

Cover art by Kenneth Turner

Betsy Wagner
P.O. Box 974
Columbus, Texas 78934
spiritofgonzales@att.net

ISBN 979-8-218-49697-5

Cover art, *Dawn of the Lone Star*, by Kenneth Turner

In 2024, artist Kenneth Turner painted this beautiful commemorative piece. The painting, *Dawn of the Lone Star*, vividly depicts the express riders departing the building now called "Independence Hall" in the village of Washington on the Brazos. Each courier would carry news of the Texas Declaration of Independence throughout the territory as the Texas Revolution broiled on. It is the perfect canopy for the poems in this book, which cover the Revolution from October 1835 until April 1836.

Contents

Illustrations

Major Battles of the Texas Revolution

INTRODUCTION

Texas history is complex. There is much to consider: the Indigenous populations, Spanish occupation, Mexico's political disruptions, and American expansion. Full veracity requires consideration of all these factors.

EARLY DEVELOPMENTS OF HUMAN POPULATIONS IN TEJAS

800 – Caddos established the village of Nacogdoches

1300 – Aztecs appeared in Southern Mexico

1400 – Aztecs expanded to Central Mexico

1520 – Spain claimed all of Mexico, called it "New Spain"

1521 – Spanish Conquistador Cortez conquered the Aztecs

From 1521 until 1821 Spain claimed all of Mexico, including all the land now known as Texas.[1] In 1685 the French briefly attempted to colonize the gulf coast, which created special Spanish focus on that area. During this time Spain built missions to convert the Indigenous people to Catholicism and to prevent the French from increasing their holdings.[2] A presidio was built near each mission to house soldiers who would protect the missionaries and anyone living or working in the missions.[3] The missions became sites of conflict, three of which are featured in the poems of this book.

MISSIONS AND PRESIDIOS ALONG THE SAN ANTONIO RIVER

1690 – Mission Espada

1718 – Mission Alamo de Valero (Alamo)

1720 – Mission San Jose

1722 – Mission Espirito Santo (Goliad)

1731 – Mission Concepcion (Siege of Bejar)

1756 – Mission San Juan Capistrano

From early October 1835 through late April 1836 men fought for control of Coahuila y Tejas. Indigenous people, Spanish "vecinos," Tejanos, Mexicans, Americans and European volunteers participated on both sides for approximately 213 days. There were victories and losses, insults and arguments, enthusiasm and hesitation. But when all the fighting was over, Texas was a Republic.

The personal accounts of select participants are condensed into simple verse for this book, describing seven months of bloody drama. The following poems will both entertain and inform students of Texas history. They are intended to honor the individuals who participated in the Texas Revolution. It is only because they recorded their experiences that we have this brief glimpse onto a stage from the past.

When the Earth was created, the land mass was one great supercontinent that scientists call "Pangea." Over the next several-hundred-million years, the great waters affected the lay of the land, and Pangea broke into the various continents on Earth. Eventually, humans appeared on the land.

The areas now known as Oklahoma, Louisiana, and Texas were home to many human groups. Among those was a group known as Caddos, who claimed to have originated in sealed underground villages where they lived until a brave leader named Moon led them out.[4] They referred to this undergound dwelling as "The Place of Crying." Their above-ground home was called "Tayshas," which meant "friends." Later, "Tayshas" became "Tejas," and finally "Texas."

Texas in the Beginning

Texas started long ago
And grew lovelier throughout history.
She came from gentle, ancient plains
Arising like a mystery.

Among the natives of her culture
In the earliest of years,
Were Caddos who called her "Tayshas"
And blessed her with their tears.

The Spanish tried to claim her.
They left, and she survived
To serve as Mexico's northland—
Then Anglo men arrived.

For fifteen years the Anglos came.
They embraced the land and toiled.
When Santa Anna defiled the law
The white men's plans were foiled.

And so they had a conflict.
It led to several fights.
Santa Anna did some things
To crush the people's rights.

The conflicts didn't take too long,
Tho' a lot of blood was spent.
I wrote the verses in this book
To tell you how it went.

By September 1835, rumors of war and rumblings of suppression had been heard in Tejas for several years. When they finally became reality, Texians were ready. The resistance started in the little village of Gonzales when the settlers refused to relinquish a cannon loaned to them a few years earlier by the Mexican government. The following poem is based on actual events recorded by men who were involved.[5]

Come and Take It

It started on a Tuesday
In October of ‘35.
Eighteen men of Gonzales —
None of whom are still alive —

Were all working together.
And now we can be sure
Their righteousness is measured
By the years the town has endured.

They kept a little cannon
Over on the village square.
In spite of Mexico’s demands
They would keep it there.

The little gun was faulty.
To shoot it was a ploy.
The Indians always feared that thing
Because of its terrible noise!

The cannon was security
For everyone around.
Although, its worse damage
Was inflicted by its sound.

But orders came from Mexico,
A note from a soldier's pack.
"Because of your disloyalty
You must give the cannon back."

Tom Miller told the waiting scout,
"You can't just take it away!
You must ask our Alcalde—
and he's not in town today."

"Then I'll come back mañana,
And we can make a plan.
My general will wait that long,"
Explained the soldier-man.

But Panton, the Alcalde,
Wasn't really far from town.
It was a trick the townsmen played
To keep the pressure down.

And so, there was a standoff.
Castañeda's men gathered 'round
To wait for Panton to return.
They camped outside the town.

Meanwhile, the Gonzales men
Rode a few miles away
To tell Panton about the threat.
They asked, "What do you say?"

"We can't do that!" Panton said.
The other men agreed.
"To surrender our defenses
Would go against our creed!"

"Let's go get other farmers!
We'll recruit from far and wide!
We need more fire power,
More guns at our side!"

The dragoons were growing restless
Just waiting for the gun.
They sent another soldier
To say what must be done.

He came on Thursday morning
To make the same demand.
With great respect, but forcefully
So Panton would understand.

"We must have that cannon back,
Kind sir, it is my duty!
The little gun is all we want.
We'll ask no other booty."

But Panton held his position.
He told the waiting man,
"Go back and tell Castañeda,
Come and take it, if he can!"

The waiting scout seemed baffled.
He glared...then turned to go.
In a voice that almost threatened,
He said, "Adiós, amigo..."

On Friday, in the morning
Each side took their place.
Neither side was willing
To give up in disgrace.

They met in Williams' farm field
To avoid the rising river.
The air was thick and cold that day.
It caused a dreadful shiver.

The Mexicans lined up in rows.
An easy target was baited!
Meanwhile, all the Texas men
Hid in the trees and waited.

Colonel Moore rode out to talk.
He said to Castañeda,
"You know, if you do not retreat,
My men will want their vendetta."

"But soldiers do what we are told,"
Castañeda said.
"I must comply or there will be
Consequences I will dread!"

So Moore reined his horse away.
Conditions now were dire.
He launched into a gallop,
Raised his hand and shouted, "FIRE!"

The cannon blew like thunder.
Shards from the blast rained down.
As always, the awful roar she made
Was heard back in the town.

The blast had its desired effect.
It caused sufficient damage.
Some blood and cries of injury
Were more than they could manage.

Castañeda realized
The Texians had him beat.
In order to avoid the worst
He organized retreat.

The Texas men let out a cheer
To realize what happened.
In spite of Mexico's demand
They kept the little cannon.

Castañeda went back home.
No victory had he won.
The Texas Revolution
Had only just begun.

COME AND TAKE IT

After the battle for the cannon in Gonzales, Mexican General Cos posted some Mexican troops in the village of San Antonio, some seventy-five miles west of Gonzales. Texian scouts learned of this occupation and reported it to Stephen Austin in San Felipe. Austin sent James Bowie and Juan Seguin to determine the best camp site for Texian volunteers to observe the situation. As this news went throughout the province of Tejas, volunteers from every village gathered in the woods around San Antonio, expecting to take siege of the town and run the Mexican squad back across the Rio Grande.

The poem "The Seige of Bexar," based on messages sent among the participants, explains this phase of the revolution.[6]

The Siege of Bexar

In the fall of '35
Because we kept our gun...
We Texians were all inspired
By the victory we had won!

But word came that soldados
Walked the streets of a town
Only seventy-five miles away!
A threat we must put down!

And so, recruits from far and wide
Made our way through the woods
To join with Austin's army
To do the best we could.

We scouted 'round the missions
And chose Concepción.
It gave the best advantage
To see what was going on.

There we camped and waited.
"We're not ready," some asserted.
But "waiting" wasn't "fighting,"
So some men deserted!

Thinking we had so few men,
Cos sent out his "best"!
In spite of our few numbers
We still would win that test!

It wasn't till December 9th
Milam said, "Let's go on out there!"
Two hundred of us followed him
As we stormed the public square.

Johnson led with Milam.
In two divisions we proceeded
Through the streets of Bexar
While the soldados retreated!

As Bowie, Fannin and Colonel Neill
Heightened their advance,
The soldados turned around and ran,
Showing nothing but their pants!

Then Cos sent out a flag of truce
To make his intentions known.
"I'll retire from this unpleasant place,
And we can all go home."

So, Cos and General Burleson
Sat down to capitulate.
With Christian generosity
We sent them on their way.

With rifles for their hunting
They left for Matamoros.
Little did we realize...
They soon would come back for us.

After the siege of Bexar, the Texians established a presence in San Antonio. Cos was required to surrender his headquarters in the 1718 Spanish Mission called El Alamo, and the Texians made their headquarters in the abandoned mission. The Texian Regular Army officers were Colonel William Travis and Colonel James C. Neill. The militia volunteers voted to have James Bowie as their commander. Neill took emergency leave to help his ailing family. In Neill's absence, Travis took control. In late February the lookout sentinel reported large columns of Mexican forces approaching El Alamo. Travis sent letters to the various villages asking for help. The village of Gonzales sent thirty-two volunteers. The following poem is dedicated to them.[7]

THE IMMORTAL THIRTY-TWO

I'll tell you of my brothers' work.
It was far from pretty.
We came and fought — and yes, we lost.
But we don't want your pity.

Albert Martin brought the news.
It riled us up to hear
The desperate plea to come and help.
So, we gathered up our gear!

We all met in Gonzales' square.
We mustered one by one.
We waited for the briefest time
To see who else might come.

"Let's head on out!" George Kimble said,
"We can't wait any longer!"
I led my mount to join the rest
Their hooves began to thunder.

We travelled hard the first two days.
We pushed to our fullest extent.
The more ambitious riders
Were Flanders and Andrew Kent.

Day 3, Squire Damon said to Floyd
That caution now was needed.
The idea grew with Cain and White,
That notion widely heeded.

Day 4, we rode a wider path.
John Garvin stalked for scouts.
Tom Miller warned, “They’ll trap our camp!”
For that we had no doubts!

And finally, on the 29th
We waited in the woods.
Jacob Darst reminded us
To be as quiet as we could.

My friend Phil King was stealthy.
He slipped up to the pen.
He got the guards' attention
And said, "Hey, let us in!"

At last, the gates were opened.
We were so cunning and bold!
We dodged the scouts from Mexico
In the early morning cold.

There we found the Texas force
Just as we expected:
Defiant, bold and vigilant
In the bastions they'd perfected.

We saw their worried faces
Reflected in the lamps.
They grabbed our gear and slapped our backs
And welcomed us to camp.

The sight of it appalled us,
Worse than Travis' letter said.
We saw mothers with their children,
And Bowie was sick in bed!

It came to our attention,
Within hours it was clear,
That Texas was in danger
Of losing everything so dear!

James George looked at Dearduff
To give him inspiration.
Concern shot through the group of us
As we questioned our migration!

Isaac Baker went into action
With Fishbaugh on his left.
They took a post atop the wall
To give the others rest.

By sunup shooting started.
From the distant guns it came.
We didn't see those cannons yet,
But they were deadly, just the same.

And from the town we heard the band.
They played the cold "Deguello."
The bugles sang their promise
To send us all to their inferno.

In spite of our resistance
Many took a hit.
The women dressed the bloody wounds
From a meager doctor's kit.

The cruel aggression wouldn't stop,
The chaos was unrelenting!
We thought we had discovered hell,
But what good was our lamenting?

They gradually encircled us,
With guns and knives and ladders.
Their cannons broke the mission walls.
Our defenses didn't matter.

So, we cloistered in the barracks.
Someone bolted the big doors.
We ran to the supply carts
And waited between the stores.

My heart was pounding in my brain.
I found it hard to breathe.
My chest was tight, and I noticed
A strange chatter in my teeth.

Soon they blew the bolted doors
And continued to pursue us!
From room to room, their masses came.
Their blades were passing through us.

Then I saw the Fuqua boy.
His young face was shattered.
His jaw was hit. He tried to speak.
He spit his blood and blathered.

John Davis tried to help his friend.
A bullet stopped his kindness.
Milsaps took one in the face,
Inflicting him with blindness.

The time went by with screams and shouts,
With punishing confusion.
The camp became a murder scene —
Sant' Anna's retribution.

I saw the bodies on the ground —
Neggan, Wright and Jackson.
As Lindley, Summers and Cottle
Kept up their valiant action.

George Tumlinson was going strong,
I thought he might survive!
But then, alas, a musket blew,
And he fell by my side.

A soldado grabbed me by my hair —
I had no more time.
I shoved my knife between his ribs
And traded his life for mine.

It went on that way for hours,
Men being sliced and shot.
Till one by one, we all were lost —
But the Mexicans were not.

The ground was like a butcher shop.
Soldados built a fire.
Their captain said to pick us up
And throw us on the pyre.

So, that's the way it ended.
For us the war was over.
Our time was short, our mission lost —
The dread of every soldier!

That was the end at the Alamo,
But surely not for Texas!
Sam Houston led another band.
Vengeance is infectious!

Did we buy time for Texas?
It darn sure wasn't free!
The time we gave old Sam was bought
By my brothers, and by me!

My name was John Gaston.
There was no one else to tell it.
Except Almaron's dear wife,
Whose courage earned her merit!

So, if you knew old Jess McCoy,
Despallier or Cummings —
Or if you knew John Kellogg
Or any of the others —

You know that they were precious
To their mothers, wives and children!
Remember us in Texas —
We're looking down from heaven.

Isaac G. Baker
John Cain
"Wash" Cottle
David P. Cummings
Jacob C. Darst
John Davis
Squire Daymon
William Dearduff
Charles Despallier
Almaron Dickinson
William Fishbaugh
John Flanders
Dolphin Ward Floyd
Galba Fuqua
John E. Garvin
John E. Gaston
James George
Thomas Jackson
John B. Kellogg II
Andrew Kent
George C. Kimble
William Philip King
Jonathan L. Lindley
Albert Martin
Jesse McCoy
Thomas R. Miller
Isaac Millsaps
George Neggan
William E. Summers
George W. Tumlinson
Robert White
Claiborne Wright
The Immortal Thirty-two

In late February of 1836, Colonel Travis sent three letters from the Alamo asking "people anywhere" for help. Only the thirty-two men from Gonzales responded. But the entire region became aware of the impending danger from the Mexican raids. From the Rio Grande going northeastward across all of Tejas to the Sabine, settlers fled in a panic. Some families near the Rio Grande left when they saw the Mexican troops amassing, while others left in March after news of the loss of the Alamo. There are many accounts of this flight. The following poem is based on the memoirs of Dilue Rose, a ten-year-old child who fled with her family from the Harrisburg area.[8]

The Runaway Scrape

Oh, look who's here, dear Mother!
It's my favorite uncle!
Your brother James, so tall and strong,
With eyes that always twinkle!

But not today, dear Mother.
His eyes are full of dread.
He says he needs some leather bags
For carrying his lead.

That letter you read yesterday,
The one from the Alamo —
It said the army needs more help.
They wanted us to know.

Uncle James says he will help,
But first he needs to tell us
Something very troubling.
James is acting nervous.

The Mexicans are angry.
They want us to go away.
And they say they will kill us
If we decide to stay.

The woods are full of soldados
Coming from Mexico.
Everyone is running away.
Uncle James says we should go.

But first James needs to get supplies
Before he meets his friends.
He says we should leave the house
Until the turmoil ends.

I'll melt some lead and mold it.
I know how it's done.
I'll make James some bullets
To help our peace get won.

I'll heat the lead and make it soft,
And scoop it with a spoon.
Uncle James will have his shot,
And he will be back soon.

Surely we can wait one day.
Maybe James is wrong.
Let's wait to hear some other news.
One day is not too long.

Papa went down to the meadow.
I thought he was going to plow.
But he took all mother's dishes
And buried them in the ground!

Look, Mother! They took our wagon!
That leaves us with none.
I think without a wagon,
We can just stay home.

It's morning now, dear Mother,
And Uncle James is gone.
The neighbors too are leaving.
Most of them left at dawn.

I watched them go, and I wondered:
Is everyone afraid?
Would Mexico really rob us
Of all the plans we made?

Papa made our farm here.
He loves this beautiful land.
Look, Mother — Papa is calling us,
And he has a note in his hand.

Papa, what now is the trouble?
He turns away moaning and shakes.
"The men have all died with Travis,"
He says in a voice that breaks.

"Soldados are coming to get us."
In his pain, Papa looks down at me.
"We have no choice but to run now.
Pack up quickly, and then we can flee."

Mama bundles the baby.
My sister is four months old.
She is sick with a fever and chills.
I hope it is only a cold.

Big sister, please come help me.
Just throw some pots on the sled.
It's starting to rain. We'd like to abstain,
But running is better than dead.

Mama has bundled our blankets.
She says, "Oh, Lord! What shall we eat?"
She opens the cupboard and brings out
Some bread and some carrots and meat.

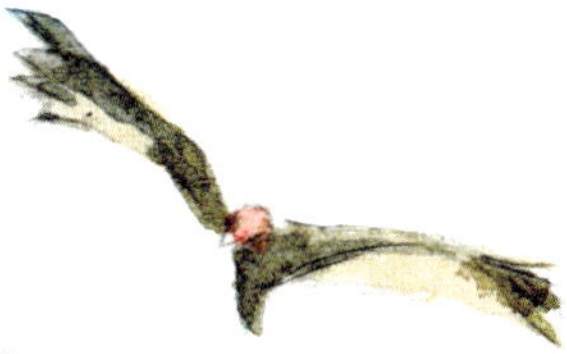

We'll take some onions and bacon.
Just enough to get us by.
Papa loads it all on the donkey's back,
And we leave the house with a sigh.

Another cold, wet day ahead.
Five families together move out.
The mud is up past our ankles,
And our neighbor limps with his gout.

We walk and trudge until midnight.
The Shipmans share our camp.
Mrs. Roark helps us with the baby.
We're soaked, and our bedding is damp.

The panic and fear are chaotic.
My thoughts are all in a swirl.
Surely this will make more sense
When I am an older girl.

The Trinity River is rising.
Thousands are waiting to cross.
The barge broke apart in the river.
I shudder to think of our loss.

Outlaws are drawn to the chaos.
Conditions for thieves are ideal.
They terrorize and panic us,
Trying to pillage and steal.

Marauders come thundering at us
Yelling, "The Mexicans are near!"
Our panic now is doubled, as if
We hadn't enough to fear!

The devils on horseback spread terror,
To make the helpless women run!
The fiends steal what the women dropped.
They laugh and shoot off their guns.

The baby is convulsing.
Blood flows from her nose.
Papa gives her minerals
And holds the baby close.

Mama is beside herself,
In helpless desperation.
Mrs. Shipman comforts Mama
'Til we reach Liberty Station.

The baby died in Papa's arms.
We buried her in the town.
For a while we'll stay behind.
Everyone is so beaten down.

Death is all around us now.
Hundreds fill the roads.
The dead are buried where they fall.
May heaven welcome their souls.

After three weeks of waiting
Papa comes with good news.
A raft is being assembled.
So we can cross over soon.

We'll stay in the river bottom
While the men assemble the raft.
At last, it is my family's turn
So we all load up on the craft.

I've lost my shoes and my bonnet.
My dress is filthy and torn.
But we push on; we can't give up
No matter how tired or worn.

As we inch our way eastward
I think of all we've lost.
And I hope that when this is over
The prize will be worth the cost.

Oh, listen! We hear cannons fire!
The thunderous vibrations are brief.
Papa says that must mean Texas is lost,
Which only adds to our grief.

As darkness settles upon us
A scout brings 'round a note.
It says that Houston has WON the war!
And we can all go home!

Papa takes charge and leads us west.
We arrive at the battleground.
The field is covered with the dead,
And vultures are all around.

The stench is such as I've never known,
And hope never to know again.
I don't know how they managed it,
But it looks like the Texans DID win!

No one is sure about it.
The women all glance in doubt.
There might be dangers in the woods —
Maybe Indians or Mexican scouts!

The King family also started for home.
Mr. King waded into the stream.
An alligator knocked him down,
And his wife began to scream.

The 'gator lunged at Mr. King —
Both went down in the mud.
My stomach was sick when we came upon
That place with the muddy blood.

I'm turning my eyes away, Mother.
I can't bear what I see.
I don't want to look at the horrors.
Will this be the end of me?

I'm revived by the courage of others,
Those brave men who fought for our homes!
What is now the REPUBLIC OF TEXAS
Was bought with their blood and their bones.

So I pick myself up and push homeward.
I think it's the least I can do.
Respecting the price of our freedom
Paid by those unfortunate few.

Oh, look! There's our house now, Mother!
Papa says we'll be there soon!
We must wait to make sure of our safety.
We'll be home by tomorrow at noon!

The morning sun is a welcome sight,
In spite of the damage we see!
The house is a-plunder, all ruined —
But "home" still looks good to me!

We left our fate to the armies.
We just wanted to survive.
Though our homes were put to the torches,
Maybe now we can really thrive!

We ran from our past to our future
Not knowing the size or the shape
Of the monster we faced in the running.
They call it the RUNAWAY SCRAPE.

In 1722 Mission Espiritu Santo was built by the Spaniards near the Indian village of Santa Dorotea, in the southeast region of Tejas, just fifty miles from the Gulf of Mexico. A presidio called La Bahia was built nearby to protect the mission and its inhabitants. Mexico inherited La Bahia when Spain left in 1821 and continued to post soldiers there. In 1829 the name of the village around the presidio was changed to Goliad.

When rumblings of Tejas' rebellion grew serious in the fall of 1835, Mexican General Cos went to Goliad. He left the presidio on October 5th, taking most of the Mexican troops with him to San Antonio. Seeing their opportunity, a small Texian force led by George Collinsworth slipped into the poorly manned presidio and overtook it on October 10th.[9]

In February of 1836 James Fannin was assigned to command Goliad. Fannin set about organizing his fort and changed the name to Fort Defiance. In March 1836 Sam Houston sent word for Fannin to destroy Fort Defiance and take his men to Victoria.[10] Fannin delayed, resulting in a massacre.

The following poem is based on the memoirs of Herman Ehrenberg, a German volunteer who survived the last maneuvers of the men of Goliad.[11]

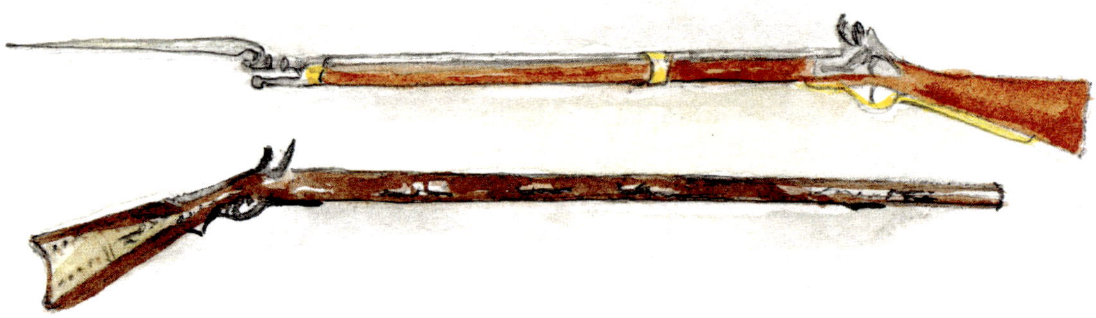

Remembering Goliad

Texas was tainted by murder and lust.
Redmen ruled there by arrows and dust.
Spaniards' lodges were quickly crushed.
        So, they built a mission at Goliad.

Then Anglos moved in for want of the land.
Austin and Houston needed more hands.
And down near Victoria in the heat and the sand
        Stood the old mission of Goliad.

We heard of this venture far away in my home
In Germany, and I was eager to roam!
So I sailed across on the ocean foam,
        Clueless of Goliad.

I went to New Orleans where I was persuaded
To join with the soldiers. By the river I waited
For the barge with the rest of the men with ill-fated
        Prospects at Goliad.

Then I crossed into Texas near Nacogdoches.
We danced in cantinas, most audacious!
And laughed at the Mexicans, so ferocious!
Not knowing of Goliad.

We made merry and drank our wine.
We invited new friends to come and dine.
We danced with the ladies, with never a sign...
Of what awaited us at Goliad.

We were proudly known as New Orleans Grays.
Eager we were to join in the fray!
To the District of Bexar, we went on our way...
Never dreaming of Goliad.

In San Antonio we teased the soldados.
When they gave up, we felt like heroes!
The ease of it caused a bloat to our egos...
But we weren't yet to Goliad.

We buried Ben Milam and one or two others.
We were saddened by the loss of these brothers.
But soldiers should know, we adventuresome lovers...
Many roads lead to Goliad.

The Grays left the city to find our next quest.
To Copano Bay and onward we pressed!
With no doubt in our minds that we were the best!
And would be...until Goliad.

After a time, Fannin's brigantine came.
His 'Bama Red Rovers would now join the game.
The Militia, the Reds, or the Grays...all the same!
We would all go to Goliad.

On through the tall prairie grasses we went.
Soon the coyotes and the wolves had our scent.
The vultures followed without even a hint
Of danger at Goliad.

Sam Houston addressed us and warned us one day.
"Destroy that mission and be on your way!"
But Fannin hesitated...he decided to stay
    In the mission at Goliad.

Fannin conflated his fears and ambition.
"We'll wait here for help!" he cried with elation.
He believed reinforcements would come to that station,
    His precious Goliad.

Fannin's choices were foolish and cruel.
The logistical training they taught him in school
Was useless in this thousand-man-duel.
    Unfitting for Goliad.

Fannin finally left, much too late.
But Urrea's soldiers didn't wait.
They surrounded Fannin's troops and closed the gate
    To the road back to Goliad.

The Mexican rifles fired through the air.
Lead balls went flying everywhere!
They landed in bodies desperate to share
The shelter of Goliad.

The night was filled with the cries of the dying.
Coyotes came while Fannin was sighing.
The expected reinforcements were still denying
The men of Goliad.

Finally, Fannin felt he had no choice.
He flew a white flag, and in his own voice
He made an arrangement to take us boys
Back to Goliad.

Colonel Holzinger made the deal.
He wrote Travis' wishes and put a seal
On a promise for us, having shown so much zeal.
They took us all back to Goliad.

We were to work in the mines with the lead.
In exchange for our work, we were to be fed.
That would be better than being dead
    And buried at Goliad!

Then other prisoners joined our band.
From Victoria and Copano they came over land.
These other captives, tied hand-to-hand
    Were brought to Goliad.

Urrea sent a letter to ask for concessions.
To murder us all was beyond his aggression.
We waited, hoping for some discretion.
    In the solution of Goliad.

Finally, Urrea received a reply.
Santa Anna had spoken from somewhere on high.
We prayed a reconciliation was nigh...
    For the prisoners of Goliad.

They lined us up and called the roll.
We formed three divisions, just as we were told.
Their jaws were tight, their attitudes cold
        As they led us from Goliad.

Not far from the gates we were told to "HALT!"
Wondering how we were at fault
We knelt in reply to their verbal assault
        Outside of Goliad.

Then all I could hear was gunfire and screams.
I lunged away from the bloody scenes!
The rifles attacked my brothers and me
        As I ran from Goliad!

I believed the river was close. I could hear it.
Its comforting waters gave me nothing to fear it.
I ran for the stream; I knew I was near it!
        I couldn't go back to Goliad!

A Mexican lancer struck my head.
He hit me and ran; he assumed I was dead.
I fell in bushes and there, as I bled...
    I resented old Goliad!

God was with me. I escaped with my life.
Others succumbed to the murder and strife.
Hearts were ripped open with bullets and knives
    On my brothers at Goliad.

In mass executions later inside the gates
Cold-hearted butchers performed their disgrace.
Fannin himself was shot in the face
    By the devils at Goliad.

But after a time their fate was avenged.
In a field near a bayou, in a slaughter of THEM
Santa Anna himself heard the cries of our men,
    "Remember Goliad!"

May the people remember for all their days
The Texan Militia, the Reds and the Grays.
Fannin's Spirit is lurking in the mist and the haze
With the men lost at Goliad.

By April 1, 1836, Mexico had challenged the Texians in San Antonio, Gonzales, Lipantitlán, San Patricio, Agua Dulce, Refugio, and Goliad.[12] Sam Houston was a strategist who practiced restraint. While many were critical of what they saw as his cowardice, Houston confidently retreated to safer prairies, waiting for the perfect set of circumstances. He led his troops, adding to their numbers and developing their skill along the way. Santa Anna sent his generals on three different routes,[13] with a plan to meet at the Brazos River and force the Texian "pirates" out of Mexico at the Sabine. For weeks both armies moved eastward. Houston was building his strength while Santa Anna's army was becoming weaker.

On April 20th Houston had his advantage. The Texians were seasoned and motivated. The following poem is based on Sam Houston's biography describing the events that finally resulted in the Republic of Texas.[14]

Victory at San Jacinto

At nine o'clock in the morning
Of April the twenty-first
The Texians at San Jacinto
Were anxious — and someone cursed.

"Look there!" he said as he watched them.
"Those scoundrels are flooding the ridge!"
Houston's a fool, and we are his tool
If we let them cross over the bridge!"

"We'll eat them alive! Don't let them survive!"
The Texians made their commitments.
"For the brothers they killed, now THEIR blood will be spilled!
That's the purpose of our enlistment!"

But Houston sat quietly, thinking his thoughts.
His silence was infuriating.
"He's a coward! We should attack!"
They said as he sat meditating.

Meanwhile, across the field
Santa Anna was flaunting his power.
His men were so sure that they would endure
The next battle, at any hour.

At ten Houston turned to "Deaf" Smith
And quietly gave a command
To chop down the bridge and block retreat.
His decision put victory at hand.

By noon a council of war was held
To consider their next move.
The officers suggested strategies but
Nothing Houston would approve.

At one the field was quiet.
Both sides held their aggression.
A siesta was held in the Mexican camp
While the Texians prepared ammunition.

Santa Anna lounged in his elegant tent
With drugs and a pretty lady.
His men took their naps, like sleepy old cats.
They dozed and became rather lazy.

This brief relaxation gave Houston his cue.
In the silence he made up his mind.
This was his chance to make his advance
And catch Santa Anna's men blind.

At three a love song filled the air,
A reminder of families and home.
It stirred the courage in their hearts
To defend the land they would own.

"Will you come to the Bower I have shaded for you?"
The words reminisced in each head.
"And the rose of your cheek shall not rival your lips..."
Well, they couldn't taste kisses if dead!

And so, through the tall grasses they crept.
Houston whispered, "Hold your fire..."
The act of delaying their vengeance
Only served to bolster their ire.

By four the Texians assaulted,
Advancing like lions on lambs.
They surprised the great leader and all those sleepers
As the final battle began.

"Remember the Alamo!" everyone cried.
"You butchered our brothers!" they yelled.
In shock and surprise the men tried to rise.
But the sleepy soldados just fell.

You killed them at Goliad! Now YOU will pay!"
The Texians cried in their rage.
Caught completely off guard, soldiers fell in the yard,
With no chance to even engage.

By nightfall the fighting was over.
A few of the Texians died.
Hundreds of dead soldados
Lay in the field side by side.

Houston's ankle was shattered.
He struggled but insisted to walk.
The Mexican officers surrendered,
And the Texians gathered to talk.

Mosley Baker said, "We owe them nothing!
We should just finish them all!
They took no prisoners at Goliad!
Just shoot them! We don't need to stall!"

But Houston wouldn't have it.
Texas was better than that.
"We'll march them off to a prison," he said.
Baker just cursed and spat.

At noon the day after the battle
A woman arrived on her land.
Peggy McCormick protested,
“These men have all died, by YOUR hand!”

“And now they are putrid and stinking!”
She pleaded her case in despair.
“My land is polluted, and you have concluded
It’s good... and you don’t even care!”

“Dear woman!” Houston addressed her.
“Your land will forever be dear
To future generations of Texans
Who’ll commemorate what took place here!”

She glared in his face and defied him.
“Get them off!” was all she could say.
As the stench in the air floated by them
They each turned and went their own way.

As he left her, he scanned the horizon.
A gray-clad division was seen
Marching with flags of concession
Toward the place where the battle had been.

General Juan Almonte
Was surrendering four hundred men.
Houston observed the surrender
And then fell in the arms of his friend.

The pain of his leg was crushing.
Doc Ewing went to work on the wound
While the Texian scouts brought in prisoners
For the rest of the afternoon.

At dusk Scout Robinson rode into camp
With a "peasant" riding behind.
The prisoner wore a coy look on his face
As if he had something in mind.

The "peasant" looked unusually healthy,
Though his clothes were ragged and loose.
He was characteristically swarthy — but weak...
And the man wore red velvet shoes!

Robinson led his horse toward the prisoners
Who were under the watch of a guard.
The man in red shoes got down from the horse
And walked to the prison yard.

"Mira! El Presidente!"
The prisoners saluted and bowed!
The man in red shoes was Sant' Anna!
And his men betrayed him out loud!

The "peasant" squared up his shoulders.
"Take me to Houston," he said.
He lifted his chin to hide his chagrin,
As he turned and looked straight ahead.

Houston invited the prisoner
To join him under a tree.
The two of them sat to negotiate.
Santa Anna asked to go free.

"But you had no mercy in Goliad,"
Houston reminded his foe.
"And you showed your thirst for Texian blood
At the mission called El Alamo."

At last Santa Anna surrendered.
He held a losing hand.
He requested his favorite barbiturate,
And consented to Houston's demands.

Then President Burnet arrived on the scene,
With Sherman and Lamar gave a cheer!
They drooled at the sight of the victory,
And spent an hour picking up souvenirs.

The politicians shunned Sam Houston
As his leg wound threatened his life.
His work was, to them, just "his duty."
They refused to acknowledge his strife.

Houston's men had complete admiration now
For what their commander had done.
But the self-serving politicians
Never acknowledged all Houston had won.

They all went off to Galveston,
Each to pursue his own goal.
Burnet and Sherman remained as friends,
Snubbing Houston as they all grew old.

Texas was now a Republic.
Her future would turn many ways.
She would be her own country
For three thousand six hundred days.

LIBERTY
OR DEATH

EPILOGUE

Texas Becomes a State —

"Only Texas could turn defeat into a legend..."[15]

While all the combatants were fighting for the Texas Republic, a committee was meeting in the village of Washington, Texas, drawing up a constitution. Independence from Mexico was declared on March 2, 1836. Couriers (see cover) carried the news across the territory as the fighting continued in the places described in the poems of this book. The final act against Santa Anna took place in a farm field in San Jacinto on April 21, 1836. At that point, Texas ruled herself. Mexico never accepted the Treaty of Velasco, and threats to reclaim the land continued.

The victory at San Jacinto was an expensive one. Texas never had the resources to function as a thriving nation should. She struggled in poverty for about nine years until the United States came to her assistance. In November of 1845, Texas citizens voted for statehood in a landslide. The United States adopted Texas on December 20th. The government of the Republic evaded that fact for several weeks more. She finally removed the Lone Star flag and replaced it with the Nation's Stars and Stripes in late February of 1846. The State of Texas would add the twenty-eighth star to that flag.

"The Republic of Texas is no more..."[16] Those were the words uttered by a conflicted President Anson Jones as Texas became the twenty-eighth state. Since that time, Texas has thrived and contributed much as a member of the greatest nation on earth: a nation created and sustained by honorable people such as those you have read about in the poems in this book.

NOTES

1. Source for history of human populations
History.com editors, "Mexico Timeline," History, January 27, 2010, https://www.history.com/topics/latin-america/mexico-timeline.

2. Source for French and Spanish colonization in Texas
"French – Spanish Rivalry in Tejas (Texas), 1685-1690," National Humanities Center, https://nationalhumanitiescenter.org/pds/amerbegin/power/text2/SpanishFrenchRivalry.pdf. Or use search terms "French - Spanish rivalry in Tejas (Texas)" in your browser's search engine.

3. Sources for Spanish missions in early Texas
Odie B. Faulk, *A Successful Failure: the Saga of Texas, 1519-1810* (Steck-Vaughn Company, 1965), 92-95.

Odie B. Faulk, *The last years of Spanish Texas, 1787-1821* (Mouton & Co., 1964), 72-74.

4. Sources for the Caddo people in Texas
Chase Kahwinhut Earles, "Caddo History & Culture," Caddo Pottery, https://www.caddopottery.com/culture.

Cody Crews, "The Caddo Tribes of Louisiana," Louisiana Encyclopedia, louisiana-anthology.org/encyclopedia/c/caddo_tribes.html.

5. Sources for "Come and Take It"
Henry Steward Foote, *Texas and the Texans*, Volume II, (Philadelphia: Cowperthwait & Co, 1941) 97-103.

Juan N. Sequín, *A Revolution Remembered: The Memoirs and Remembrances of Juan N. Sequín* (Austin: Texas State Historical Association, 2002), 105.

6. Sources for "The Siege of Bexar"
"Muster at Gonzales, Siege and Battle of Bexar, October 3-December 11, 1835," Sons of Dewitt Colony Texas, https://www.sonsofdewittcolony.org/musterbexar.htm.

Sequín, *A Revolution Remembered: The Memoirs and Remembrances of Juan N. Sequín*, 196.

7. Source for "The Immortal Thirty-Two"
William Fairfax Gray, *Diary of Col. Wm. Fairfax Gray: From Virginia to Texas 1835-36* (Houston: Fletcher Young Publishing Company, 1965), 136-141.

8. Source for "The Runaway Scrape"
Jo Ella Exley, *Texas Tears and Texas Sunshine* (College Station: Texas A&M University Press, 1985), 54-74.

9. Sources for George Collinsworth taking Goliad
News staff, "Collinsworth Lead Victory at 1st Battle at Goliad," Bay City Sentinel, June 22, 2023.

Bill and Marjorie K. Walraven, *The Magnificent Barbarians: Little Told Tales of the Texas Revolution* (Austin: Eakin Press, 1993), 34-36.

10. Sources for Fannin ignoring Sam Houston's orders to leave Goliad
Bill and Marjorie K. Walraven, *The Magnificent Barbarians*, 82-85.

Sam W. Haynes, *Unsettled Land: From Revolution to Republic, the Struggle for Texas* (New York: Basic Books, 2022), 192.

11. Source for "Remembering Goliad"
James E. Crisp, editor, with assistance from Louise E. Brister, and translated by Louise E. Brister, with the assistance of James C. Kearney, *Inside The Texas Revolution: The Enigmatic Memoir of Herman Ehrenberg* (Austin: Texas State Historical Association, 2001-2003), 202-336.

12. Source for "By April 1, 1836, Mexico had challenged the Texians..."
Bill and Marjorie K. Walraven, *The Magnificent Barbarians*, iv.

13. Source for "Santa Anna sent his generals on three different routes..."
Marquis James, *The Raven: A Biography of Sam Houston* (University of Texas Press, 1929 and 2013), map of campaigns showing routs of various generals (insert).

14. Source for "Victory at San Jacinto"
Marquis James, *The Raven*, 238-257.

15. Source for quote, "Only Texas could turn defeat into a legend..."
Rosemary Kent, *The Genuine Texas Handbook*, (New York: Workman Publishing Company, 1987), 147.

16. Source for quote, "The Republic of Texas is no more..."
Joe B. Franz, *Texas: A History* (New York: W.W. Norton & Company, 1984), 87.

About the Author

Betsy Wagner retired from a career in education in 2008. Her work took her to classrooms and administrative positions in Texas, Louisiana, Hawaii, and Germany. It was about the time of her retirement that she first learned of her father's ancestors' participation in the Texas Revolution. She began researching the facts of that participation and discovered the things revealed in her first two books, *Spirit of Gonzales* and *Dauntless Spirit.*

In 2022 she completed a third historical novel, *German Spirit for Texas Freedom*, about her mother's German ancestors.

In 2023 she published the book *The Immortal Thirty-Two*, which was written for a memorial event held at the Alamo to honor the Gonzales Ranging Troops who came to Travis' call for help.

Her fifth book, *Spirits of The Texas Revolution*, is a collection of seven poems which span the full scope of the Texas Revolution.

Betsy lives in Columbus, Texas. The town is a vestige of Texas history, one of the earliest colonies settled by Stephen Austin in 1821. She can be contacted through her website, www.someplacedownintexas.com.

About the Illustrator

Susan Walrath Pape knew her love for art at an early age. Her parents encouraged her, as they shared this appreciation of art and music. Her first job was working at a local offset printing company, which she began in high school and continued through college. After graduation from Skidmore College in 1977 she took a job with a Boston design firm, specializing in educational publishing. She worked her way through the ranks to become the Associate Art Director with Prentice-Hall Educational Division. She moved to Texas in 2001, earned her Texas teacher certification, and taught art at Cypress-Fairbanks ISD middle school.

Sue has worked in oils, watercolors, acrylics, and alcohol inks. She is retired from teaching and now lives in La Grange where she continues to teach for Arts for Rural Texas (ARTS) in Fayette County. She is a member of Daughters of the American Revolution, American Women Artists, Live Oak Art Center in Columbus, Texas, Lost Pines Art Center in Bastrop, Texas, and OPS-Outdoor Painters Society. Sue participates in various art shows around the state and can be contacted through her website, www.biddieranchart.com.

About the Cover Artist

Kenneth Turner has been an artist since childhood. He won the Westbury High School Art Scholarship award in 1966. He majored in Fine Arts at the University of Houston. Ken studied alongside Lajos Markos, a Hungarian artist who trained at the Royal Academy of Budapest. Markos' love for painting animals, especially horses, brought him to Texas. He mentored Ken for three years, pushing Ken's skill to a new level. Ken's excellence in capturing the physical elegance, graceful movement and value of service of the horse is displayed in his painting *Dawn of the Lone Star*, the cover of this book.

Ken has painted for families all over the world. His paintings have memorialized historic events in Texas and the United States. His excellent work can be seen in Houston's First Baptist Church, the George H. W. Bush Presidential Library and Museum in College Station, the Ronald Reagan National Airport, the New York City Police Museum, the New York City Fire Department, and the headquarters of the Port Authority of New York and New Jersey. He has painted portraits of such notables as Rick Perry, Ben Carson, Bud Adams, Judge Robert Eckels, David and Eula Winterman, Dan Crenshaw, and many others. Ken Turner can be contacted through his website, https://kennethturnerart.com.

Made in the USA
Columbia, SC
29 September 2024

db4ad2f7-1f88-4085-a9d1-1dcfae8bc63aR01